WIN THE MORNING, WIN THE DAY

A Daily-Weekly-Monthly Gratitude Journal
Designed to Help You Conquer Life-Changing Goals

Raelyn Stevenson

Editorial Project Management: Karen Rowe, www.karenrowe.com
Cover Design: Antonio Garcia, thisisagm.com
Inside Layout: Ljiljana Pavkov

Printed in the United States

ISBN: 978-1-7777174-0-7 (hardcover)

To those who want more in life.

The path to change unfolds one step at a time. Congratulations on taking the first step! Your journey to a healthier, happier, more successful life starts today.

"You can keep talking yourself out of the thing you're hoping for, or you can decide that your dream is more powerful than your excuse."

—RACHEL HOLLIS

INTRODUCTION

Welcome to your *Win the Morning, Win the Day* gratitude journal! Congratulations on the start of your new daily ritual that will help you conquer your life-changing goals. Until now, you have probably always dreamt of what your life would be like once you lost the weight, paid off the debt, bought the house, got the dream job or improved your mental health. I am here to tell you that your dream can become your reality.

After years of struggling to lose unwanted weight and be happy with myself, I had eventually given up hope. It felt as though I'd been proving to myself time and time again that I could *not* achieve my goal. From dieting, training, running a half marathon and everything in between, I could not seem to lose the weight. Feeling defeated, I decided to buy a gratitude journal, not to help me lose the weight but to help me feel better about myself. Lo and behold, the results were life-changing. Cliché I know, but that is the honest truth and what originally sparked my passion for journaling.

Journaling has since become part of my life; like brushing my teeth, I journal religiously every morning. Before journaling, I was not a morning person. I would smash that snooze button for a couple more minutes of shut eye before forcing myself to wake up. Now, I wake up intentionally two hours earlier as part of my morning routine.

Journaling allowed me to conquer my unachievable goals by helping me adjust my mindset. Through journaling, I changed my mindset and ultimately changed my results. If you don't already know, you are what you tell yourself and you can accomplish ANYTHING you set your mind to! That was my missing puzzle piece. Journaling allowed me to shift my mindset while keeping my focus and vision clear on what it was I wanted to achieve. The end result for me was losing 25 lbs and conquering my life-changing goal.

Life changing is an understatement. Thanks to journaling, my entire outlook on life has changed. I have changed my daily routine, created healthy habits and improved my mindset and overall quality of life.

My original goal was to lose weight, but once I changed my mindset, weight loss just became an additional bonus to my newfound energy and excitement for life. Journaling allowed me to see this when I found myself expressing gratitude for increased productivity, better sleep quality, and improved quality of life instead of the number on the scale.

I think that's why I love journaling so much: it allowed me to remain focused on my Primary Goal while avoiding tunnel vision so I could enjoy the benefits and **struggles** along the way. Not to mention once I achieved my Primary Goal of becoming healthier and losing 25 lbs, I then revisited my goals and picked a new Primary Goal: *create a gratitude journal*.

After accomplishing the goal I never thought I could, I realized the sky is the limit and I can achieve anything I set my mind to. I started holding myself to a higher expectation in all areas of my life and began setting goals for my health, finance, career and relationships. Overall, these areas flourished with this process and I know the same will happen for you when you decide your dreams are more powerful than your excuses.

Good Luck,

Raelyn

HOW IT WORKS

This journal will only work if you do.

The first step is to be extremely clear, precise, and explicit when it comes to what it is you want to achieve. Once you have visualized this, write it down. This is your Primary Goal. Studies have shown that those who write down their goals are 10 times more likely to achieve them, and I couldn't agree more!

Your *Primary Goal* is what you are going to be consistent with every single day until it is complete. By journaling and acknowledging your Primary Goal daily, you will never lose focus on what it is you are going to achieve. This will require extreme self-discipline and commitment and it will be essential to challenge your comfort zones and limiting beliefs while taking the required steps towards your Primary Goal. Eventually these small daily steps will compound and become life–changing.

This journal will assist you with creating daily, weekly, and monthly habits to achieve your most desired goals in all areas of your life. During this process, you will have regular check-ins to reflect your progress in order to keep you on track and accountable.

To begin, set your monthly goals in Finance, Career, Relationships, Health and Fitness that you would like to achieve in the upcoming month while documenting your Primary Goal in the top right corner. If you are unsure which goal you would like to be your Primary Goal, write down the goals you would like to achieve in these four areas and pick one to be your Primary Goal. There are some examples of each area below. If five goals in each area seems overwhelming feel free to leave some blank and start small.

From here, break down your monthly goals into smaller steps you can take throughout the week to get you closer to your Primary Goal. I would recommend starting on a Sunday by setting your goals for the week ahead. You can also reference and utilize your weekly reflection habit tracker throughout the week starting on page 30 and at the end of every week.

Now you're ready to begin practicing daily journaling. This will include daily gratitude, setting your expectation for the day and writing your daily affirmations to keep you focused on your Primary Goal. Daily gratitude starts with listing three things you are grateful for each morning. I love this process! Expressing gratitude is the best way to start the day because you realize the small things *are* the big things and that during some of your darkest days you can always find things to be grateful for. Because you do this every day, these three things do not have to be huge; I am often grateful for a good night's sleep, a good cup of coffee or a compliment I received at work.

Although at times your daily goals may not directly influence your Primary Goal, this will increase your overall productivity. For example, if your top priorities to accomplish throughout the day include folding the laundry, making a healthy meal, and paying your bills, you might be wondering how accomplishing these will get you closer to your Primary Goal. But if not having clean clothes, healthy food in the fridge or the bills paid on time is taking up your time, space, or energy then by completing these tasks you are allowing more of your energy to go towards what really matters: *your Primary Goal*.

If you are unfamiliar with affirmations, they are part of the practice of positive thinking for self-empowerment. To do this, you will need to create a positive affirmation suitable to your goal. Your daily affirmation defines who you want to be or what you want to achieve. I recommend writing your daily affirmations as if you have already achieved the goal. As I mentioned above, you are what you tell yourself so by telling yourself you are what you want to achieve you are that much more likely to achieve it.

Examples of daily affirmations include:

> *I am debt free.*
> *I am confident in who I am as a person.*
> *I am capable of anything I set my mind to.*
> *I am now 20 pounds lighter and feeling wonderful.*
> *I own my dream home.*
> *I am now assistant manager.*
> *I own my own business.*
> *I own a rental property.*
> *I have a healthy relationship.*
> *I save 10% of my income a month.*

You may find this process repetitive so remember the keys to achieving any goal are adjusting the process so it is catered for your own success. In simple terms, I use this space to write down whatever encouragement I may need for that specific day. For instance, "I invest in myself, therefore my investment returns an abundance of wealth," or "good things happen to me because I do good things for others," or "I am capable of anything I set my mind to," or "I am having a productive day." Those are among my favourite daily affirmations, and I like them because they always keep me in a positive and abundant mindset. Take this opportunity to get creative and use this space for whatever encourages you.

Remember, this is an ongoing process and there is *always* room for improvement. This is not a one and done; this is a lifestyle. Everyone is moving towards their Primary Goals at different speeds. Once you have prioritized and completed one Primary Goal, select a new one and start the process over again. **Below is a detailed example of how the entire process works.**

"Your entire life can really change in a year. You just gotta love yourself enough to know you deserve more, be brave enough to demand more, and be disciplined enough to actually work for more."

—Unknown

EXAMPLE

Primary Goal: Buy a House.
Monthly Goal: Create a monthly budget to manage spending and ensure saving a sufficient down payment for home purchase.
Weekly Goal: Meal prep for the week ahead to avoid overspending.
Daily Goal: Eat lunches prepared and monitor spending.

Date

February 1, 2021

Primary Goal:

Buy a House

Month: February

Goals for this Month:

HEALTH & FITNESS
1. Drink half my body weight in ounces every day
2. Exercise for 30 minutes, five days a week
3. Achieve 10,000 steps a day
4. Go to a spin class
5. No drinking pop this month

RELATIONSHIPS
1. FaceTime Grandma in long-term care
2. Spend a night at Grandpa's cabin
3. Complete past due training
4. Talk to my manager about a raise
5. Review work pension and benefits

FINANCE
1. Save 10% of my income this month
2. Get a combined quote to save money
3. Pay off my credit card in full
4. Create a budget
5. Book an appointment for a mortgage pre-approval

CAREER
1. Finish month-end reports
2. Meet sales targets for the month
3. Invite neighbours for coffee
4. Attend group exercise classes once a week
5. Plan drinks one night after work with colleges

OTHER
1. Three hours or less of screen time a day
2. Finish painting office
3. Take the bottles in
4. Read a book
5. Try a new recipe for supper

WEEKLY GOALS

Date   **Primary Goal:**

February 1, 2021   Buy a House

Week: January 31-February 7th

Goals for this Week:

What goals do I want to accomplish this week to get me closer to my primary goal?

1. Prepare meals for the week ahead

2. Follow my prepared finance budget

3. Exercise five out of seven days this week

4. Drink 60 ounces of water everyday

5. Attend an exercise class

6. Less than three hours of screen time a day

7. Achieve 10,000 steps a day

Day 1/7

Date

February 1, 2021

Primary Goal:

Buy a House

*"We cannot change what we are not aware of,
and once we are aware, we cannot help but change."*

—SHERYL SANDBERG

Four things that I am grateful for:

1) A good cup of coffee this morning

2) Setting my goals and intentions for the week ahead

3) My half-hour walk in the sun yesterday

4) Quality time with family

What would I do differently from yesterday that my future self would thank me for?

I would have been more mindful of my water intake. Yesterday I did not get my water intake and as a result I had a headache. I would have woken up earlier so I had time to enjoy journaling before work yesterday morning.

Where did I win yesterday?

After supper I went for a half-hour walk in the sunshine. I also had less than three hours of screen time which is within my acceptable range.

What are my three goals to accomplish today? If this is all I get accomplished today I will be happy and three steps closer towards my primary goal.

1. Achieve 10,000 steps

2. Drink 60 ounces of water

3. Read my book before bed

"The best way to predict your future is to create it"

Daily Affirmations (as if you have already achieved it):

1. I bought a home

2. I have a $15,000 down payment saved

3. I am capable of anything I set my mind to

"We cannot become what we want by remaining what we are."

—Max Depree

Date

February 1, 2021

Primary Goal:

Buy a House

Weekly Goal Tracker

Week of: January 31-February 7th

Goal	Mon	Tue	Wed	Thu	Fri	Sat	Sun
Prepare meals for the week ahead							Y
Follow my prepared finance budget	Y	Y	Y				
Exercise five out of seven days	Y	Y		Y	Y	Y	
Drink 60 ounces of water a day	Y	Y	Y	Y	Y	Y	Y
Attend an exercise class						Y	
Less than three hours of screen time daily	Y	Y	Y	Y	Y	Y	Y
Achieve 10,000 steps a day	Y	Y	Y	Y	Y		

Out of the goals you set last week, how many did you accomplish successfully?
5 / 7 .

Congratulations on the goals you accomplished successfully! You are that much closer to achieving your Primary Goal! Make sure you take the time to praise yourself for what you have accomplished and how far you have come.

Where did I win last week?

1) I prepared meals for the week which resulted in me not buying lunch once

2) I achieved 10,000 steps everyday

3) I took the bottles in —one of my monthly goals

4) I received an unexpected wage increase last week

How can I improve next week?

1) Keep screen time below three hours/day

2) Drink less coffee to ensure getting my water intake daily

3) Wake up earlier to exercise in the mornings

4) Continue meal prepping on Sundays

5) Book an appointment for a mortgage pre-approval

Let's get started!

Now that you have seen an example of the entire process, it's time to start working towards *your* goals. Remember, what works for one person may not work for you. Feel free to be creative and make adjustments so that this process is tailored for your success. All that matters is that you start!

"One day or day one: you decide."

—#LIVEWITHMEANING

MONTH:

Date   **Primary Goal:**

Month:

Goals for this Month:

HEALTH & FITNESS

1. ....
2. ....
3. ....
4. ....
5. ....

FINANCE

1. ....
2. ....
3. ....
4. ....
5. ....

RELATIONSHIPS

1. ....
2. ....
3. ....
4. ....
5. ....

CAREER

1. ....
2. ....
3. ....
4. ....
5. ....

OTHER

1. ....
2. ....
3. ....
4. ....
5. ....

WEEK ONE

Date   **Primary Goal:**

Week:

Goals for this Week:

What goals do I want to accomplish this week to get me closer to my
Primary Goal?

1. ....

2. ....

3. ....

4. ....

5. ....

6. ....

7. ....

You can document your weekly goals on your habit tracker pages at the end
of every week to review your success.

Day 1/7

Date: **Primary Goal:**

*"We cannot change what we are not aware of,
and once we are aware, we cannot help but change."*

—SHERYL SANDBERG

Four things that I am grateful for:

1) ....

2) ....

3) ....

4) ....

What would I do differently from yesterday that my future self would thank me for?

....

Where did I win yesterday?

....

What are my three goals to accomplish today? If this is all I get accomplished today I will be happy and three steps closer towards my Primary Goal.

1) ....

2) ....

3) ....

"The best way to predict your future is to create it"

Daily Affirmations (as if you have already achieved it):

1) ....

2) ....

3) ....

Day 2/7

Date: **Primary Goal:**

"A beautiful day begins
with a beautiful mindset."

—UNKNOWN

Four things that I am grateful for:

1) ....

2) ....

3) ....

4) ....

What would I do differently from yesterday that my future self would thank me for?

....

Where did I win yesterday?

....

What are my three goals to accomplish today? If this is all I get accomplished today I will be happy and three steps closer towards my Primary Goal.

1) ....

2) ....

3) ....

"The best way to predict your future is to create it"

Daily Affirmations (as if you have already achieved it):

1) ....

2) ....

3) ....

Day 3/7

Date: **Primary Goal:**

> *"Either you run the day,*
> *or the day runs you."*
>
> —JIM ROHN

Four things that I am grateful for:

1) ....

2) ....

3) ....

4) ....

What would I do differently from yesterday that my future self would thank me for?

....

Where did I win yesterday?

....

What are my three goals to accomplish today? If this is all I get accomplished today I will be happy and three steps closer towards my Primary Goal.

1) ....

2) ....

3) ....

> *"The best way to predict your future is to create it"*

Daily Affirmations (as if you have already achieved it):

1) ....

2) ....

3) ....

Day 4/7

Date: **Primary Goal:**

"Happiness is not a goal...
it's a by-product of a life well lived."

—ELEANOR ROOSEVELT

Four things that I am grateful for:

1) ....

2) ....

3) ....

4) ....

What would I do differently from yesterday that my future self would thank me for?

....

Where did I win yesterday?

....

What are my three goals to accomplish today? If this is all I get accomplished today I will be happy and three steps closer towards my Primary Goal.

1) ....

2) ....

3) ....

"The best way to predict your future is to create it"

Daily Affirmations (as if you have already achieved it):

1) ....

2) ....

3) ....

Day 5/7

Date: **Primary Goal:**

> *"If you really want to do something, you'll find a way.*
> *If you don't, you'll find an excuse."*
>
> —JIM ROHN

Four things that I am grateful for:

1) ....

2) ....

3) ....

4) ....

What would I do differently from yesterday that my future self would thank me for?

....

Where did I win yesterday?

....

What are my three goals to accomplish today? If this is all I get accomplished today I will be happy and three steps closer towards my Primary Goal.

1) ....

2) ....

3) ....

"The best way to predict your future is to create it"

Daily Affirmations (as if you have already achieved it):

1) ....

2) ....

3) ....

Day 6/7

Date: **Primary Goal:**

"When you do what is easy, life is hard.
When you do what is hard, life is easy."

—Patrick Rurka

Four things that I am grateful for:

1) ....

2) ....

3) ....

4) ....

What would I do differently from yesterday that my future self would thank me for?

....

Where did I win yesterday?

....

What are my three goals to accomplish today? If this is all I get accomplished today I will be happy and three steps closer towards my Primary Goal.

1) ....

2) ....

3) ....

"The best way to predict your future is to create it"

Daily Affirmations (as if you have already achieved it):

1) ....

2) ....

3) ....

Day 7/7

Date: **Primary Goal:**

*"If you can learn to love yourself and all the flaws,
you can love other people so much better."*

—KRISTIN CHENOWETH

Four things that I am grateful for:

1) ....

2) ....

3) ....

4) ....

What would I do differently from yesterday that my future self would thank me for?

....

Where did I win yesterday?

....

What are my three goals to accomplish today? If this is all I get accomplished today I will be happy and three steps closer towards my Primary Goal.

1) ....

2) ....

3) ....

"The best way to predict your future is to create it"

Daily Affirmations (as if you have already achieved it):

1) ....

2) ....

3) ....

Weekly Reflection

*"We cannot become what we want
by remaining what we are."*

—Max Depree

Date: **Primary Goal:**

Weekly Goal Tracker

Week of: ....

Goal	Mon	Tue	Wed	Thu	Fri	Sat	Sun

Out of the goals you set last week, how many did you accomplish successfully?

.................../.................. .

Congratulations on the goals you accomplished successfully! You are that much closer to achieving your Primary Goal! Make sure you take the time to praise yourself for what you have accomplished and how far you have come.

Where did I win last week?

1)

2)

3)

4)

5)

How can I improve next week?

"It does not matter how slowly you go as long as you do not stop."

—CONFUCIUS

WEEK TWO

Weekly Goals   **Primary Goal:**

Week:
Goals for this Week:

What goals do I want to accomplish this week to get me closer to my Primary Goal?

1. ....

2. ....

3. ....

4. ....

5. ....

6. ....

7. ....

You can document your weekly goals on your habit tracker pages at the end of every week to review your success.

Day 1/7

Date: **Primary Goal:**

"Being okay if it happens and okay if it doesn't is a very powerful place to be."

—KATE ECKMAN

Four things that I am grateful for:

1) ....

2) ....

3) ....

4) ....

What would I do differently from yesterday that my future self would thank me for?

....

Where did I win yesterday?

....

What are my three goals to accomplish today? If this is all I get accomplished today I will be happy and three steps closer towards my Primary Goal.

1) ....

2) ....

3) ....

"The best way to predict your future is to create it"

Daily Affirmations (as if you have already achieved it):

1) ....

2) ....

3) ....

Date: **Primary Goal:**

"Believe you can and you're halfway there."

– THEODORE ROOSEVELT

Four things that I am grateful for:

1) ....

2) ....

3) ....

4) ....

What would I do differently from yesterday that my future self would thank me for?

....

Where did I win yesterday?

....

What are my three goals to accomplish today? If this is all I get accomplished today I will be happy and three steps closer towards my Primary Goal.

1) ....

2) ....

3) ....

"The best way to predict your future is to create it"

Daily Affirmations (as if you have already achieved it):

1) ....

2) ....

3) ....

Day 3/7

Date: **Primary Goal:**

> *"Life is a gift, and it offers us the privilege, opportunity, and responsibility to give something back by becoming more."*
>
> – TONY ROBBINS

Four things that I am grateful for:

1)

2)

3)

4)

What would I do differently from yesterday that my future self would thank me for?

Where did I win yesterday?

What are my three goals to accomplish today? If this is all I get accomplished today I will be happy and three steps closer towards my Primary Goal.

1)

2)

3)

> *"The best way to predict your future is to create it"*

Daily Affirmations (as if you have already achieved it):

1)

2)

3)

Day 4/7

Date: **Primary Goal:**

"Cultivate an optimistic mind, use your imagination, always consider alternatives, and dare to believe that you can make possible what others think is impossible."

—RODOLFO COSTA

Four things that I am grateful for:

1) ....

2) ....

3) ....

4) ....

What would I do differently from yesterday that my future self would thank me for?

....

Where did I win yesterday?

....

What are my three goals to accomplish today? If this is all I get accomplished today I will be happy and three steps closer towards my Primary Goal.

1) ....

2) ....

3) ....

"The best way to predict your future is to create it"

Daily Affirmations (as if you have already achieved it):

1) ....

2) ....

3) ....

Day 5/7

Date: **Primary Goal:**

"Be the kind of person who dares to face life's challenges and overcome them rather than dodging them."

—ROY T. BENNETT

Four things that I am grateful for:

1) ....

2) ....

3) ....

4) ....

What would I do differently from yesterday that my future self would thank me for?

....

Where did I win yesterday?

....

What are my three goals to accomplish today? If this is all I get accomplished today I will be happy and three steps closer towards my Primary Goal.

1) ....

2) ....

3) ....

"The best way to predict your future is to create it"

Daily Affirmations (as if you have already achieved it):

1) ....

2) ....

3) ....

Day 6/7

Date: **Primary Goal:**

"Everything is within your power,
and your power is within you."

—JANICE TRACHTMAN

Four things that I am grateful for:

1) ....

2) ....

3) ....

4) ....

What would I do differently from yesterday that my future self would thank me for?

....

Where did I win yesterday?

....

What are my three goals to accomplish today? If this is all I get accomplished today I will be happy and three steps closer towards my Primary Goal.

1) ....

2) ....

3) ....

"The best way to predict your future is to create it"

Daily Affirmations (as if you have already achieved it):

1) ....

2) ....

3) ....

Day 7/7

Date: **Primary Goal:**

*"The difference in winning and losing is most often...
not quitting."*

—WALT DISNEY

Four things that I am grateful for:

1) ....

2) ....

3) ....

4) ....

What would I do differently from yesterday that my future self would thank me for?

....

Where did I win yesterday?

....

What are my three goals to accomplish today? If this is all I get accomplished today I will be happy and three steps closer towards my Primary Goal.

1) ....

2) ....

3) ....

"The best way to predict your future is to create it"

Daily Affirmations (as if you have already achieved it):

1) ....

2) ....

3) ....

WEEKLY REFLECTION

"We cannot become what we want by remaining what we are."

—Max Depree

Date: **Primary Goal:**

WEEKLY GOAL TRACKER

Week of: ....

Goal	Mon	Tue	Wed	Thu	Fri	Sat	Sun

Out of the goals you set last week, how many did you accomplish successfully?

.................../.................. .

Congratulations on the goals you accomplished successfully! You are that much closer to achieving your Primary Goal! Make sure you take the time to praise yourself for what you have accomplished and how far you have come.

Where did I win last week?

1) ....

2) ....

3) ....

4) ....

5) ....

How can I improve next week?

....

....

....

....

....

"The best time to plant a tree was 20 years ago.
The second-best time is now."

—Chinese Proverb

WEEK THREE

Weekly Goals   **Primary Goal:**

Week:

Goals for this Week:

What goals do I want to accomplish this week to get me closer to my Primary Goal?

1. ....

2. ....

3. ....

4. ....

5. ....

6. ....

7. ....

You can document your weekly goals on your habit tracker pages at the end of every week to review your success.

Day 1/7

Date: **Primary Goal:**

*"Being okay if it happens and okay if it doesn't
is a very powerful place to be."*

—KATE ECKMAN

Four things that I am grateful for:

1) ....

2) ....

3) ....

4) ....

What would I do differently from yesterday that my future self would thank me for?

....

Where did I win yesterday?

....

What are my three goals to accomplish today? If this is all I get accomplished today I will be happy and three steps closer towards my Primary Goal.

1) ....

2) ....

3) ....

"The best way to predict your future is to create it"

Daily Affirmations (as if you have already achieved it):

1) ....

2) ....

3) ....

Day 2/7

Date: **Primary Goal:**

"You can, you should,
and if you're brave enough to start, you will."

—STEPHEN KING

Four things that I am grateful for:

1) ....

2) ....

3) ....

4) ....

What would I do differently from yesterday that my future self would thank me for?

....

Where did I win yesterday?

....

What are my three goals to accomplish today? If this is all I get accomplished today I will be happy and three steps closer towards my Primary Goal.

1) ....

2) ....

3) ....

"The best way to predict your future is to create it"

Daily Affirmations (as if you have already achieved it):

1) ....

2) ....

3) ....

Day 3/7

Date: **Primary Goal:**

"Success is a state of mind. If you want success,
start thinking of yourself as a success."

—DR. JOYCE BROTHERS

Four things that I am grateful for:

1) ....

2) ....

3) ....

4) ....

What would I do differently from yesterday that my future self would thank me for?

....

Where did I win yesterday?

....

What are my three goals to accomplish today? If this is all I get accomplished today I will be happy and three steps closer towards my Primary Goal.

1) ....

2) ....

3) ....

"The best way to predict your future is to create it"

Daily Affirmations (as if you have already achieved it):

1) ....

2) ....

3) ....

Date: **Primary Goal:**

"Gratitude helps you to grow and expand; gratitude brings joy and laughter into your life and into the lives of all those around you."

—Eileen Caddy

Four things that I am grateful for:

1) ....

2) ....

3) ....

4) ....

What would I do differently from yesterday that my future self would thank me for?

....

Where did I win yesterday?

....

What are my three goals to accomplish today? If this is all I get accomplished today I will be happy and three steps closer towards my Primary Goal.

1) ....

2) ....

3) ....

"The best way to predict your future is to create it"

Daily Affirmations (as if you have already achieved it):

1) ....

2) ....

3) ....

Day 5/7

Date: **Primary Goal:**

> *"The most common way people give up their power is by thinking they don't have any."*
>
> —ALICE WALKER

Four things that I am grateful for:

1) ....

2) ....

3) ....

4) ....

What would I do differently from yesterday that my future self would thank me for?

....

Where did I win yesterday?

....

What are my three goals to accomplish today? If this is all I get accomplished today I will be happy and three steps closer towards my Primary Goal.

1) ....

2) ....

3) ....

> *"The best way to predict your future is to create it"*

Daily Affirmations (as if you have already achieved it):

1) ....

2) ....

3) ....

Day 6/7

Date: **Primary Goal:**

"The greatest discovery of all time is that a person can change her future by merely changing her attitude."

—OPRAH WINFREY

Four things that I am grateful for:

1) ....

2) ....

3) ....

4) ....

What would I do differently from yesterday that my future self would thank me for?

....

Where did I win yesterday?

....

What are my three goals to accomplish today? If this is all I get accomplished today I will be happy and three steps closer towards my Primary Goal.

1) ....

2) ....

3) ....

"The best way to predict your future is to create it"

Daily Affirmations (as if you have already achieved it):

1) ....

2) ....

3) ....

Day 7/7

Date: **Primary Goal:**

"Develop an attitude of gratitude, and give thanks for everything that happens to you, knowing that every step forward is a step toward achieving something bigger and better than your current situation."

—BRIAN TRACY

Four things that I am grateful for:

1)

2)

3)

4)

What would I do differently from yesterday that my future self would thank me for?

Where did I win yesterday?

What are my three goals to accomplish today? If this is all I get accomplished today I will be happy and three steps closer towards my Primary Goal.

1)

2)

3)

"The best way to predict your future is to create it"

Daily Affirmations (as if you have already achieved it):

1)

2)

3)

WEEKLY REFLECTION

"We cannot become what we want by remaining what we are."

—MAX DEPREE

Date: **Primary Goal:**

WEEKLY GOAL TRACKER

Week of: ....

Goal	Mon	Tue	Wed	Thu	Fri	Sat	Sun

Out of the goals you set last week, how many did you accomplish successfully?

.... / ....

Congratulations on the goals you accomplished successfully! You are that much closer to achieving your Primary Goal! Make sure you take the time to praise yourself for what you have accomplished and how far you have come.

Where did I win last week?

1) ....

2) ....

3) ....

4) ....

5) ....

How can I improve next week?

....

....

....

....

....

"Isn't it nice to think that tomorrow is a new day with no mistakes in it yet?"

—L.M. MONTGOMERY

WEEK FOUR

Weekly Goals   **Primary Goal:**

Week:

Goals for this Week:

What goals do I want to accomplish this week to get me closer to my Primary Goal?

1. ....

2. ....

3. ....

4. ....

5. ....

6. ....

7. ....

You can document your weekly goals on your habit tracker pages at the end of every week to review your success.

Day 1/7

Date: **Primary Goal:**

"Taking care of yourself is productive."

—@MYSELFLOVESUPPLY

Four things that I am grateful for:

1) ....

2) ....

3) ....

4) ....

What would I do differently from yesterday that my future self would thank me for?

....

Where did I win yesterday?

....

What are my three goals to accomplish today? If this is all I get accomplished today I will be happy and three steps closer towards my Primary Goal.

1) ....

2) ....

3) ....

"The best way to predict your future is to create it"

Daily Affirmations (as if you have already achieved it):

1) ....

2) ....

3) ....

Date: **Primary Goal:**

"Gratitude is one of the strongest and most transformative states of being. It shifts your perspective from lack to abundance and allows you to focus on the good in your life, which in turn pulls more goodness into your reality."

—JEN SINCERO

Four things that I am grateful for:

1) ....

2) ....

3) ....

4) ....

What would I do differently from yesterday that my future self would thank me for?

....

Where did I win yesterday?

....

What are my three goals to accomplish today? If this is all I get accomplished today I will be happy and three steps closer towards my Primary Goal.

1) ....

2) ....

3) ....

"The best way to predict your future is to create it"

Daily Affirmations (as if you have already achieved it):

1) ....

2) ....

3) ....

Day 3/7

Date: **Primary Goal:**

*"Whatever the mind of man can conceive and believe,
it can achieve."*

—NAPOLEON HILL

Four things that I am grateful for:

1) ....

2) ....

3) ....

4) ....

What would I do differently from yesterday that my future self would thank me for?

....

Where did I win yesterday?

....

What are my three goals to accomplish today? If this is all I get accomplished today I will be happy and three steps closer towards my Primary Goal.

1) ....

2) ....

3) ....

"The best way to predict your future is to create it"

Daily Affirmations (as if you have already achieved it):

1) ....

2) ....

3) ....

Day 4/7

Date: **Primary Goal:**

"Our greatest weakness lies in giving up. The most certain way to succeed is always to try just one more time."

—Thomas Edison

Four things that I am grateful for:

1)

2)

3)

4)

What would I do differently from yesterday that my future self would thank me for?

Where did I win yesterday?

What are my three goals to accomplish today? If this is all I get accomplished today I will be happy and three steps closer towards my Primary Goal.

1)

2)

3)

"The best way to predict your future is to create it"

Daily Affirmations (as if you have already achieved it):

1)

2)

3)

Day 5/7

Date: **Primary Goal:**

> *"Choose the positive. You have a choice. You are the master of
> your attitude. Choose the positive, the constructive."*
>
> —BRUCE LEE

Four things that I am grateful for:

1) ....

2) ....

3) ....

4) ....

What would I do differently from yesterday that my future self would thank me for?

....

Where did I win yesterday?

....

What are my three goals to accomplish today? If this is all I get accomplished today I will be happy and three steps closer towards my Primary Goal.

1) ....

2) ....

3) ....

> *"The best way to predict your future is to create it"*

Daily Affirmations (as if you have already achieved it):

1) ....

2) ....

3) ....

Day 6/7

Date: **Primary Goal:**

"I live by two words: tenacity and gratitude."

—Henry Winkler

Four things that I am grateful for:

1) ....

2) ....

3) ....

4) ....

What would I do differently from yesterday that my future self would thank me for?

....

Where did I win yesterday?

....

What are my three goals to accomplish today? If this is all I get accomplished today I will be happy and three steps closer towards my Primary Goal.

1) ....

2) ....

3) ....

"The best way to predict your future is to create it"

Daily Affirmations (as if you have already achieved it):

1) ....

2) ....

3) ....

Day 7/7

Date: **Primary Goal:**

"Our beliefs about what we are and what we can be precisely determine what we can be."

—TONY ROBBINS

Four things that I am grateful for:

1) ....

2) ....

3) ....

4) ....

What would I do differently from yesterday that my future self would thank me for?

....

Where did I win yesterday?

....

What are my three goals to accomplish today? If this is all I get accomplished today I will be happy and three steps closer towards my Primary Goal.

1) ....

2) ....

3) ....

"The best way to predict your future is to create it"

Daily Affirmations (as if you have already achieved it):

1) ....

2) ....

3) ....

WEEKLY REFLECTION

"We cannot become what we want by remaining what we are."

—Max Depree

Date: **Primary Goal:**

Weekly Goal Tracker

Week of: ....

Goal	Mon	Tue	Wed	Thu	Fri	Sat	Sun

Out of the goals you set last week, how many did you accomplish successfully?

.................../................... .

Congratulations on the goals you accomplished successfully! You are that much closer to achieving your Primary Goal! Make sure you take the time to praise yourself for what you have accomplished and how far you have come.

Where did I win last week?

1) ....

2) ....

3) ....

4) ....

5) ....

How can I improve next week?

....

....

....

....

....

"Whatever you do or dream you can do —begin it. Boldness has genius and power and magic in it."

—JOHANN WOLFGANG VON GOETHE

MONTH:

Date   **Primary Goal:**

Month:

Goals for this Month:

HEALTH & FITNESS

1. ....

2. ....

3. ....

4. ....

5. ....

FINANCE

1. ....

2. ....

3. ....

4. ....

5. ....

RELATIONSHIPS

1. ....

2. ....

3. ....

4. ....

5. ....

CAREER

1. ....

2. ....

3. ....

4. ....

5. ....

OTHER

1. ....

2. ....

3. ....

4. ....

5. ....

WEEK ONE

Date   **Primary Goal:**

Week:

Goals for this Week:

What goals do I want to accomplish this week to get me closer to my
Primary Goal?

1. ....

2. ....

3. ....

4. ....

5. ....

6. ....

7. ....

You can document your weekly goals on your habit tracker pages at the end
of every week to review your success.

Day 1/7

Date: **Primary Goal:**

"Gratitude unlocks the fullness of life. It turns what we have into enough, and more. It turns denial into acceptance, chaos to order, confusion to clarity. It can turn a meal into a feast, a house into a home, a stranger into a friend."

—MELODY BEATTIE

Four things that I am grateful for:

1) ....

2) ....

3) ....

4) ....

What would I do differently from yesterday that my future self would thank me for?

....

Where did I win yesterday?

....

What are my three goals to accomplish today? If this is all I get accomplished today I will be happy and three steps closer towards my Primary Goal.

1) ....

2) ....

3) ....

"The best way to predict your future is to create it"

Daily Affirmations (as if you have already achieved it):

1) ....

2) ....

3) ....

Day 2/7

Date: **Primary Goal:**

"When you complain, you make yourself a victim. Leave the situation, change the situation or accept it. All else is madness."

—Eckhart Tolle

Four things that I am grateful for:

1) ....

2) ....

3) ....

4) ....

What would I do differently from yesterday that my future self would thank me for?

....

Where did I win yesterday?

....

What are my three goals to accomplish today? If this is all I get accomplished today I will be happy and three steps closer towards my Primary Goal.

1) ....

2) ....

3) ....

"The best way to predict your future is to create it"

Daily Affirmations (as if you have already achieved it):

1) ....

2) ....

3) ....

Day 3/7

Date: **Primary Goal:**

"There is only one corner of the universe you can be certain of improving, and that's your own self."

—ALDOUS HUXLEY

Four things that I am grateful for:

1) ....

2) ....

3) ....

4) ....

What would I do differently from yesterday that my future self would thank me for?

....

Where did I win yesterday?

....

What are my three goals to accomplish today? If this is all I get accomplished today I will be happy and three steps closer towards my Primary Goal.

1) ....

2) ....

3) ....

"The best way to predict your future is to create it"

Daily Affirmations (as if you have already achieved it):

1) ....

2) ....

3) ....

Day 4/7

Date: **Primary Goal:**

*"Change your life today. Don't gamble on the future,
act now, without delay."*

—SIMONE DE BEAUVOIR

Four things that I am grateful for:

1) ....

2) ....

3) ....

4) ....

What would I do differently from yesterday that my future self would thank me for?

....

Where did I win yesterday?

....

What are my three goals to accomplish today? If this is all I get accomplished today I will be happy and three steps closer towards my Primary Goal.

1) ....

2) ....

3) ....

"The best way to predict your future is to create it"

Daily Affirmations (as if you have already achieved it):

1) ....

2) ....

3) ....

Day 5/7

Date: **Primary Goal:**

"In order to succeed, we must first believe that we can."

—Nikos Kazantzakis

Four things that I am grateful for:

1) ....

2) ....

3) ....

4) ....

What would I do differently from yesterday that my future self would thank me for?

....

Where did I win yesterday?

....

What are my three goals to accomplish today? If this is all I get accomplished today I will be happy and three steps closer towards my Primary Goal.

1) ....

2) ....

3) ....

"The best way to predict your future is to create it"

Daily Affirmations (as if you have already achieved it):

1) ....

2) ....

3) ....

Day 6/7

Set your goals high, and don't stop till you get there.

—Bo Jackson

Four things that I am grateful for:

1) ....

2) ....

3) ....

4) ....

What would I do differently from yesterday that my future self would thank me for?

....

Where did I win yesterday?

....

What are my three goals to accomplish today? If this is all I get accomplished today I will be happy and three steps closer towards my Primary Goal.

1) ....

2) ....

3) ....

"The best way to predict your future is to create it"

Daily Affirmations (as if you have already achieved it):

1) ....

2) ....

3) ....

Day 7/7

Date: **Primary Goal:**

"Life is not easy for any of us. But what of that? We must have perseverance and above all confidence in ourselves. We must believe that we are gifted for something and that this thing must be attained."

—MARIE CURIE

Four things that I am grateful for:

1) ....
2) ....
3) ....
4) ....

What would I do differently from yesterday that my future self would thank me for?

....

Where did I win yesterday?

....

What are my three goals to accomplish today? If this is all I get accomplished today I will be happy and three steps closer towards my Primary Goal.

1) ....
2) ....
3) ....

"The best way to predict your future is to create it"

Daily Affirmations (as if you have already achieved it):

1) ....
2) ....
3) ....

WEEKLY REFLECTION

"We cannot become what we want by remaining what we are."

—MAX DEPREE

Date:

Primary Goal:

WEEKLY GOAL TRACKER

Week of: ....

Goal	Mon	Tue	Wed	Thu	Fri	Sat	Sun

Out of the goals you set last week, how many did you accomplish successfully?

.... / ....

Congratulations on the goals you accomplished successfully! You are that much closer to achieving your Primary Goal! Make sure you take the time to praise yourself for what you have accomplished and how far you have come.

Where did I win last week?

1) ....

2) ....

3) ....

4) ....

5) ....

How can I improve next week?

....

....

....

....

....

"It always seems impossible until it's done."

—NELSON MANDELA

WEEK TWO

Date **Primary Goal:**

Week:

Goals for this Week:

What goals do I want to accomplish this week to get me closer to my Primary Goal?

1. ....

2. ....

3. ....

4. ....

5. ....

6. ....

7. ....

You can document your weekly goals on your habit tracker pages at the end of every week to review your success.

Day 1/7

Date: **Primary Goal:**

"Never give up on a dream just because of the time it will take to accomplish it. The time will pass anyway."

—EARL NIGHTINGALE

Four things that I am grateful for:

1) ....

2) ....

3) ....

4) ....

What would I do differently from yesterday that my future self would thank me for?

....

Where did I win yesterday?

....

What are my three goals to accomplish today? If this is all I get accomplished today I will be happy and three steps closer towards my Primary Goal.

1) ....

2) ....

3) ....

"The best way to predict your future is to create it"

Daily Affirmations (as if you have already achieved it):

1) ....

2) ....

3) ....

Day 2/7

Date: **Primary Goal:**

"Do not fear failure but rather fear not trying."

—Roy T. Bennett

Four things that I am grateful for:

1) ....

2) ....

3) ....

4) ....

What would I do differently from yesterday that my future self would thank me for?

....

Where did I win yesterday?

....

What are my three goals to accomplish today? If this is all I get accomplished today I will be happy and three steps closer towards my Primary Goal.

1) ....

2) ....

3) ....

"The best way to predict your future is to create it"

Daily Affirmations (as if you have already achieved it):

1) ....

2) ....

3) ....

Day 3/7

Date: **Primary Goal:**

"Writing in a journal reminds you of your goals and of your learning in life. It offers a place where you can hold a deliberate, thoughtful conversation with yourself."

—ROBIN SHARMA

Four things that I am grateful for:

1)

2)

3)

4)

What would I do differently from yesterday that my future self would thank me for?

Where did I win yesterday?

What are my three goals to accomplish today? If this is all I get accomplished today I will be happy and three steps closer towards my Primary Goal.

1)

2)

3)

"The best way to predict your future is to create it"

Daily Affirmations (as if you have already achieved it):

1)

2)

3)

Day 4/7

Date: **Primary Goal:**

"What we achieve inwardly will change outer reality."

—PLUTARCH

Four things that I am grateful for:

1) ....

2) ....

3) ....

4) ....

What would I do differently from yesterday that my future self would thank me for?

....

Where did I win yesterday?

....

What are my three goals to accomplish today? If this is all I get accomplished today I will be happy and three steps closer towards my Primary Goal.

1) ....

2) ....

3) ....

"The best way to predict your future is to create it"

Daily Affirmations (as if you have already achieved it):

1) ....

2) ....

3) ....

Day 5/7

Date: **Primary Goal:**

*"If you go to work on your goals, your goals will go to work on you.
If you go to work on your plan, your plan will go to work on you.
Whatever good things we build end up building us."*

—JIM ROHN

Four things that I am grateful for:

1)
2)
3)
4)

What would I do differently from yesterday that my future self would thank me for?

Where did I win yesterday?

What are my three goals to accomplish today? If this is all I get accomplished today I will be happy and three steps closer towards my Primary Goal.

1)
2)
3)

"The best way to predict your future is to create it"

Daily Affirmations (as if you have already achieved it):

1)
2)
3)

Day 6/7

Date: **Primary Goal:**

"Give yourself a gift of five minutes of contemplation in awe of everything you see around you. Go outside and turn your attention to the many miracles around you. This five-minute-a-day regimen of appreciation and gratitude will help you to focus your life in awe."

— WAYNE DYER

Four things that I am grateful for:

1) ....

2) ....

3) ....

4) ....

What would I do differently from yesterday that my future self would thank me for?

....

Where did I win yesterday?

....

What are my three goals to accomplish today? If this is all I get accomplished today I will be happy and three steps closer towards my Primary Goal.

1) ....

2) ....

3) ....

"The best way to predict your future is to create it"

Daily Affirmations (as if you have already achieved it):

1) ....

2) ....

3) ....

Day 7/7

Date: **Primary Goal:**

"Gratitude makes sense of our past, brings peace for today, and creates a vision for tomorrow."

—MELODY BEATTIE

Four things that I am grateful for:

1) ....

2) ....

3) ....

4) ....

What would I do differently from yesterday that my future self would thank me for?

....

Where did I win yesterday?

....

What are my three goals to accomplish today? If this is all I get accomplished today I will be happy and three steps closer towards my Primary Goal.

1) ....

2) ....

3) ....

"The best way to predict your future is to create it"

Daily Affirmations (as if you have already achieved it):

1) ....

2) ....

3) ....

WEEKLY REFLECTION

"We cannot become what we want by remaining what we are."

—Max Depree

Date: **Primary Goal:**

Weekly Goal Tracker

Week of: ....

Goal	Mon	Tue	Wed	Thu	Fri	Sat	Sun

Out of the goals you set last week, how many did you accomplish successfully?

.... / ....

Congratulations on the goals you accomplished successfully! You are that much closer to achieving your Primary Goal! Make sure you take the time to praise yourself for what you have accomplished and how far you have come.

Where did I win last week?

1) ....

2) ....

3) ....

4) ....

5) ....

How can I improve next week?

....

....

....

....

....

*"Perseverance is not a long race;
it is many short races one after the other."*

—WALTER ELLIOT

WEEK THREE

Date   **Primary Goal:**

Week:

Goals for this Week:

What goals do I want to accomplish this week to get me closer to my Primary Goal?

1. ....

2. ....

3. ....

4. ....

5. ....

6. ....

7. ....

You can document your weekly goals on your habit tracker pages at the end of every week to review your success.

Day 1/7

Date: **Primary Goal:**

> *"I don't have to chase extraordinary moments to find happiness —it's right in front of me if I'm paying attention and practicing gratitude."*

> —BRENE BROWN

Four things that I am grateful for:

1) ....

2) ....

3) ....

4) ....

What would I do differently from yesterday that my future self would thank me for?

....

Where did I win yesterday?

....

What are my three goals to accomplish today? If this is all I get accomplished today I will be happy and three steps closer towards my Primary Goal.

1) ....

2) ....

3) ....

> *"The best way to predict your future is to create it"*

Daily Affirmations (as if you have already achieved it):

1) ....

2) ....

3) ....

Day 2/7

Date: **Primary Goal:**

"By taking the time to stop and appreciate who you are and what you've achieved —and perhaps learned through a few mistakes, stumbles and losses —you actually can enhance everything about you. Self-acknowledgment and appreciation are what give you the insights and awareness to move forward toward higher goals and accomplishments."

—JACK CANFIELD

Four things that I am grateful for:

1) ....

2) ....

3) ....

4) ....

What would I do differently from yesterday that my future self would thank me for?

....

Where did I win yesterday?

....

What are my three goals to accomplish today? If this is all I get accomplished today I will be happy and three steps closer towards my Primary Goal.

1) ....

2) ....

3) ....

"The best way to predict your future is to create it"

Daily Affirmations (as if you have already achieved it):

1) ....

2) ....

3) ....

Day 3/7

Date: **Primary Goal:**

> *"A winner is someone who recognizes his God-given talents,*
> *works his tail off to develop them into skills,*
> *and uses these skills to accomplish his goals."*
>
> —LARRY BIRD

Four things that I am grateful for:

1)

2)

3)

4)

What would I do differently from yesterday that my future self would thank me for?

Where did I win yesterday?

What are my three goals to accomplish today? If this is all I get accomplished today I will be happy and three steps closer towards my Primary Goal.

1)

2)

3)

> *"The best way to predict your future is to create it"*

Daily Affirmations (as if you have already achieved it):

1)

2)

3)

Day 4/7

Date: **Primary Goal:**

"People with clear, written goals, accomplish far more in a shorter period of time than people without them could ever imagine."

—BRIAN TRACY

Four things that I am grateful for:

1) ....

2) ....

3) ....

4) ....

What would I do differently from yesterday that my future self would thank me for?

....

Where did I win yesterday?

....

What are my three goals to accomplish today? If this is all I get accomplished today I will be happy and three steps closer towards my Primary Goal.

1) ....

2) ....

3) ....

"The best way to predict your future is to create it"

Daily Affirmations (as if you have already achieved it):

1) ....

2) ....

3) ....

Day 5/7

Date: **Primary Goal:**

*"Dream high, beyond the sky; no matter wings so small,
keep vision bright; just dare to learn, for you are born to fly."*

—JORDAN HOECHLIN

Four things that I am grateful for:

1) ....

2) ....

3) ....

4) ....

What would I do differently from yesterday that my future self would thank me for?

....

Where did I win yesterday?

....

What are my three goals to accomplish today? If this is all I get accomplished today I will be happy and three steps closer towards my Primary Goal.

1) ....

2) ....

3) ....

"The best way to predict your future is to create it"

Daily Affirmations (as if you have already achieved it):

1) ....

2) ....

3) ....

Day 6/7

Date: **Primary Goal:**

"Nothing is impossible, the word itself says 'I'm possible'!"

—AUDREY HEPBURN

Four things that I am grateful for:

1) ....

2) ....

3) ....

4) ....

What would I do differently from yesterday that my future self would thank me for?

....

Where did I win yesterday?

....

What are my three goals to accomplish today? If this is all I get accomplished today I will be happy and three steps closer towards my Primary Goal.

1) ....

2) ....

3) ....

"The best way to predict your future is to create it"

Daily Affirmations (as if you have already achieved it):

1) ....

2) ....

3) ....

Day 7/7

Date: **Primary Goal:**

> *"I am not a product of my circumstances.*
> *I am a product of my decisions."*
>
> —STEPHEN COVEY

Four things that I am grateful for:

1) ....

2) ....

3) ....

4) ....

What would I do differently from yesterday that my future self would thank me for?

....

Where did I win yesterday?

....

What are my three goals to accomplish today? If this is all I get accomplished today I will be happy and three steps closer towards my Primary Goal.

1) ....

2) ....

3) ....

> *"The best way to predict your future is to create it"*

Daily Affirmations (as if you have already achieved it):

1) ....

2) ....

3) ....

WEEKLY REFLECTION

"We cannot become what we want by remaining what we are."

—Max Depree

Date: Primary Goal:

Weekly Goal Tracker

Week of: ....

Goal	Mon	Tue	Wed	Thu	Fri	Sat	Sun

Out of the goals you set last week, how many did you accomplish successfully?

.... / ....

Congratulations on the goals you accomplished successfully! You are that much closer to achieving your Primary Goal! Make sure you take the time to praise yourself for what you have accomplished and how far you have come.

Where did I win last week?

1) ....

2) ....

3) ....

4) ....

5) ....

How can I improve next week?

....

....

....

....

....

"With the new day comes new strength and new thoughts."

—ELEANOR ROOSEVELT

WEEK FOUR

Weekly Goals   **Primary Goal:**

Week:

Goals for this Week:

What goals do I want to accomplish this week to get me closer to my Primary Goal?

1. ....

2. ....

3. ....

4. ....

5. ....

6. ....

7. ....

You can document your weekly goals on your habit tracker pages at the end of every week to review your success.

Day 1/7

Date: **Primary Goal:**

*"You may be the only person left who believes in you,
but it's enough. It takes just one star to pierce
a universe of darkness. Never give up."*

—RICHELLE E. GOODRICH

Four things that I am grateful for:

1) ....

2) ....

3) ....

4) ....

What would I do differently from yesterday that my future self would thank me for?

....

Where did I win yesterday?

....

What are my three goals to accomplish today? If this is all I get accomplished today I will be happy and three steps closer towards my Primary Goal.

1) ....

2) ....

3) ....

"The best way to predict your future is to create it"

Daily Affirmations (as if you have already achieved it):

1) ....

2) ....

3) ....

Day 2/7

Date: **Primary Goal:**

"Gratitude is the healthiest of all human emotions. The more you express gratitude for what you have, the more likely you will have even more to express gratitude for."

—Zig Ziglar

Four things that I am grateful for:

1) ....

2) ....

3) ....

4) ....

What would I do differently from yesterday that my future self would thank me for?

....

Where did I win yesterday?

....

What are my three goals to accomplish today? If this is all I get accomplished today I will be happy and three steps closer towards my Primary Goal.

1) ....

2) ....

3) ....

"The best way to predict your future is to create it"

Daily Affirmations (as if you have already achieved it):

1) ....

2) ....

3) ....

Day 3/7

Date: **Primary Goal:**

"If you don't design your own life plan, chances are you'll fall into someone else's plan. And guess what they have planned for you? Not much."

—JIM ROHN

Four things that I am grateful for:

1)

2)

3)

4)

What would I do differently from yesterday that my future self would thank me for?

Where did I win yesterday?

What are my three goals to accomplish today? If this is all I get accomplished today I will be happy and three steps closer towards my Primary Goal.

1)

2)

3)

"The best way to predict your future is to create it"

Daily Affirmations (as if you have already achieved it):

1)

2)

3)

Day 4/7

Date: **Primary Goal:**

*I don't believe you have to be better than everybody else. I believe
you have to be better than you ever thought you could be.*

—KEN VENTURI

Four things that I am grateful for:

1) ....

2) ....

3) ....

4) ....

What would I do differently from yesterday that my future self would
thank me for?

....

Where did I win yesterday?

....

What are my three goals to accomplish today? If this is all I get accomplished
today I will be happy and three steps closer towards my Primary Goal.

1) ....

2) ....

3) ....

"The best way to predict your future is to create it"

Daily Affirmations (as if you have already achieved it):

1) ....

2) ....

3) ....

Day 5/7

Date: **Primary Goal:**

*"Your positive action combined with positive
thinking results in success."*

—SHIV KHERA

Four things that I am grateful for:

1) ....

2) ....

3)...

4)...

What would I do differently from yesterday that my future self would
thank me for?

....

Where did I win yesterday?

....

What are my three goals to accomplish today? If this is all I get accomplished
today I will be happy and three steps closer towards my Primary Goal.

1) ....

2) ....

3) ....

"The best way to predict your future is to create it"

Daily Affirmations (as if you have already achieved it):

1) ....

2) ....

3) ....

Day 6/7

Date: **Primary Goal:**

*"Stay focused, go after your dreams
and keep moving toward your goals."*

—LL Cool J

Four things that I am grateful for:

1) ....

2) ....

3) ....

4) ....

What would I do differently from yesterday that my future self would
thank me for?

....

Where did I win yesterday?

....

What are my three goals to accomplish today? If this is all I get accomplished
today I will be happy and three steps closer towards my Primary Goal.

1) ....

2) ....

3) ....

"The best way to predict your future is to create it"

Daily Affirmations (as if you have already achieved it):

1) ....

2) ....

3) ....

Day 7/7

Date: **Primary Goal:**

"Successful people maintain a positive focus in life no matter what is going on around them. They stay focused on their past successes rather than their past failures, and on the next action steps they need to take to get them closer to the fulfillment of their goals rather than all the other distractions that life presents to them."

—JACK CANFIELD

Four things that I am grateful for:

1)
2)
3)
4)

What would I do differently from yesterday that my future self would thank me for?

Where did I win yesterday?

What are my three goals to accomplish today? If this is all I get accomplished today I will be happy and three steps closer towards my Primary Goal.

1)
2)
3)

"The best way to predict your future is to create it"

Daily Affirmations (as if you have already achieved it):

1)
2)
3)

WEEKLY REFLECTION

"We cannot become what we want by remaining what we are."

—MAX DEPREE

Date: **Primary Goal:**

WEEKLY GOAL TRACKER

Week of: ....

Goal	Mon	Tue	Wed	Thu	Fri	Sat	Sun

Out of the goals you set last week, how many did you accomplish successfully?

.... / ....

Congratulations on the goals you accomplished successfully! You are that much closer to achieving your Primary Goal! Make sure you take the time to praise yourself for what you have accomplished and how far you have come.

Where did I win last week?

1) ....
2) ....
3) ....
4) ....
5) ....

How can I improve next week?

1) ....
2) ....
3) ....
4) ....
5) ....

"Courage doesn't always roar, sometimes it's the quiet voice at the end of the day whispering, 'I will try again tomorrow'."

—MARY ANNE RADMACHER

MONTH:

Date   **Primary Goal:**

Month:

Goals for this Month:

HEALTH & FITNESS

1. ....
2. ....
3. ....
4. ....
5. ....

FINANCE

1. ....
2. ....
3. ....
4. ....
5. ....

RELATIONSHIPS

1. ....
2. ....
3. ....
4. ....
5. ....

CAREER

1. ....
2. ....
3. ....
4. ....
5. ....

OTHER

1. ....
2. ....
3. ....
4. ....
5. ....

WEEK ONE

Weekly Goals   **Primary Goal:**

Week:

Goals for this Week:

What goals do I want to accomplish this week to get me closer to my Primary Goal?

1. ....

2. ....

3. ....

4. ....

5. ....

6. ....

7. ....

You can document your weekly goals on your habit tracker pages at the end of every week to review your success.

Day 1/7

Date: **Primary Goal:**

"Gratitude is riches. Complaint is poverty."

—DORIS DAY

Four things that I am grateful for:

1) ....

2) ....

3) ....

4) ....

What would I do differently from yesterday that my future self would thank me for?

....

Where did I win yesterday?

....

What are my three goals to accomplish today? If this is all I get accomplished today I will be happy and three steps closer towards my Primary Goal.

1) ....

2) ....

3) ....

"The best way to predict your future is to create it"

Daily Affirmations (as if you have already achieved it):

1) ....

2) ....

3) ....

Day 2/7

Date: **Primary Goal:**

*"When you know in your bones that your body is a sacred gift,
you move in the world with an effortless grace.
Gratitude and humility rise up spontaneously."*

—DEBBIE FORD

Four things that I am grateful for:

1) ....
2) ....
3) ....
4) ....

What would I do differently from yesterday that my future self would thank me for?

....

Where did I win yesterday?

....

What are my three goals to accomplish today? If this is all I get accomplished today I will be happy and three steps closer towards my Primary Goal.

1) ....
2) ....
3) ....

"The best way to predict your future is to create it"

Daily Affirmations (as if you have already achieved it):

1) ....
2) ....
3) ....

Day 3/7

Date: **Primary Goal:**

> *"Failure will never overtake me if my determination*
> *to succeed is strong enough."*

—OG MANDINO

Four things that I am grateful for:

1)

2)

3)

4)

What would I do differently from yesterday that my future self would thank me for?

Where did I win yesterday?

What are my three goals to accomplish today? If this is all I get accomplished today I will be happy and three steps closer towards my Primary Goal.

1)

2)

3)

> *"The best way to predict your future is to create it"*

Daily Affirmations (as if you have already achieved it):

1)

2)

3)

Day 4/7

Date: **Primary Goal:**

"'Enough' is a feast."

—BUDDHIST PROVERB

Four things that I am grateful for:

1) ....

2) ....

3) ....

4) ....

What would I do differently from yesterday that my future self would thank me for?

....

Where did I win yesterday?

....

What are my three goals to accomplish today? If this is all I get accomplished today I will be happy and three steps closer towards my Primary Goal.

1) ....

2) ....

3) ....

"The best way to predict your future is to create it"

Daily Affirmations (as if you have already achieved it):

1) ....

2) ....

3) ....

Day 5/7

Date: **Primary Goal:**

"The key to success is action,
and the essential in action is perseverance."

—SUN YAT-SEN

Four things that I am grateful for:

1)

2)

3)

4)

What would I do differently from yesterday that my future self would thank me for?

Where did I win yesterday?

What are my three goals to accomplish today? If this is all I get accomplished today I will be happy and three steps closer towards my Primary Goal.

1)

2)

3)

"The best way to predict your future is to create it"

Daily Affirmations (as if you have already achieved it):

1)

2)

3)

Day 6/7

Date: **Primary Goal:**

"You control your future, your destiny. What you think about comes about. By recording your dreams and goals on paper, you set in motion the process of becoming the person you most want to be. Put your future in good hands —your own."

—MARK VICTOR HANSEN

Four things that I am grateful for:

1)
2)
3)
4)

What would I do differently from yesterday that my future self would thank me for?

Where did I win yesterday?

What are my three goals to accomplish today? If this is all I get accomplished today I will be happy and three steps closer towards my Primary Goal.

1)
2)
3)

"The best way to predict your future is to create it"

Daily Affirmations (as if you have already achieved it):

1)
2)
3)

Day 7/7

Date: **Primary Goal:**

"What you get by achieving your goals is not as important as what you become by achieving your goals." Zig Ziglar

Four things that I am grateful for:

1) ....

2) ....

3) ....

4) ....

What would I do differently from yesterday that my future self would thank me for?

....

Where did I win yesterday?

....

What are my three goals to accomplish today? If this is all I get accomplished today I will be happy and three steps closer towards my Primary Goal.

1) ....

2) ....

3) ....

"The best way to predict your future is to create it"

Daily Affirmations (as if you have already achieved it):

1) ....

2) ....

3) ....

WEEKLY REFLECTION

"We cannot become what we want by remaining what we are."

—MAX DEPREE

Date: Primary Goal:

WEEKLY GOAL TRACKER

Week of: ....

Goal	Mon	Tue	Wed	Thu	Fri	Sat	Sun

Out of the goals you set last week, how many did you accomplish successfully?

.... / ....

Congratulations on the goals you accomplished successfully! You are that much closer to achieving your Primary Goal! Make sure you take the time to praise yourself for what you have accomplished and how far you have come.

Where did I win last week?

1) ....

2) ....

3) ....

4) ....

5) ....

How can I improve next week?

1) ....

2) ....

3) ....

4) ....

5) ....

"There is no substitute for hard work. Never give up. Never stop believing. Never stop fighting."

—HOPE HICKS

WEEK TWO

Weekly Goals   **Primary Goal:**

Week:
Goals for this Week:

What goals do I want to accomplish this week to get me closer to my Primary Goal?

1. ....

2. ....

3. ....

4. ....

5. ....

6. ....

7. ....

You can document your weekly goals on your habit tracker pages at the end of every week to review your success.

Day 1/7

Date: **Primary Goal:**

> *"Documenting little details of your everyday life becomes a celebration of who you are."*
>
> —CAROLYN V. HAMILTON

Four things that I am grateful for:

1) ....

2) ....

3) ....

4) ....

What would I do differently from yesterday that my future self would thank me for?

....

Where did I win yesterday?

....

What are my three goals to accomplish today? If this is all I get accomplished today I will be happy and three steps closer towards my Primary Goal.

1) ....

2) ....

3) ....

> *"The best way to predict your future is to create it"*

Daily Affirmations (as if you have already achieved it):

1) ....

2) ....

3) ....

Date: **Primary Goal:**

"Gratitude can transform common days into thanksgivings, turn routine jobs into joy, and change ordinary opportunities into blessings."

—WILLIAM ARTHUR WARD

Four things that I am grateful for:

1)

2)

3)

4)

What would I do differently from yesterday that my future self would thank me for?

Where did I win yesterday?

What are my three goals to accomplish today? If this is all I get accomplished today I will be happy and three steps closer towards my Primary Goal.

1)

2)

3)

"The best way to predict your future is to create it"

Daily Affirmations (as if you have already achieved it):

1)

2)

3)

Day 3/7

Date: **Primary Goal:**

"You just can't beat the person who never gives up."

—BABE RUTH

Four things that I am grateful for:

1) ....

2) ....

3) ....

4) ....

What would I do differently from yesterday that my future self would thank me for?

....

Where did I win yesterday?

....

What are my three goals to accomplish today? If this is all I get accomplished today I will be happy and three steps closer towards my Primary Goal.

1) ....

2) ....

3) ....

"The best way to predict your future is to create it"

Daily Affirmations (as if you have already achieved it):

1) ....

2) ....

3) ....

Day 4/7

Date: **Primary Goal:**

"If what you are doing is not moving you towards your goals, then it's moving you away from your goals."

—BRIAN TRACY

Four things that I am grateful for:

1) ....

2) ....

3) ....

4) ....

What would I do differently from yesterday that my future self would thank me for?

....

Where did I win yesterday?

....

What are my three goals to accomplish today? If this is all I get accomplished today I will be happy and three steps closer towards my Primary Goal.

1) ....

2) ....

3) ....

"The best way to predict your future is to create it"

Daily Affirmations (as if you have already achieved it):

1) ....

2) ....

3) ....

Day 5/7

Date: **Primary Goal:**

"If you look at what you have in life, you'll always have more. If you look at what you don't have in life, you'll never have enough."

—OPRAH WINFREY

Four things that I am grateful for:

1) ....

2) ....

3) ....

4) ....

What would I do differently from yesterday that my future self would thank me for?

....

Where did I win yesterday?

....

What are my three goals to accomplish today? If this is all I get accomplished today I will be happy and three steps closer towards my Primary Goal.

1) ....

2) ....

3) ....

"The best way to predict your future is to create it"

Daily Affirmations (as if you have already achieved it):

1) ....

2) ....

3) ....

Day 6/7

Date: **Primary Goal:**

*"The only person you are destined to become
is the person you decide to be."*

—RALPH WALDO EMERSON

Four things that I am grateful for:

1) ....

2) ....

3) ....

4) ....

What would I do differently from yesterday that my future self would thank me for?

....

Where did I win yesterday?

....

What are my three goals to accomplish today? If this is all I get accomplished today I will be happy and three steps closer towards my Primary Goal.

1) ....

2) ....

3) ....

"The best way to predict your future is to create it"

Daily Affirmations (as if you have already achieved it):

1) ....

2) ....

3) ....

Day 7/7

Date: **Primary Goal:**

"Don't quit. Never give up trying to build the world you can see, even if others can't see it. Listen to your drum and your drum only. It's the one that makes the sweetest sound."

—SIMON SINEK

Four things that I am grateful for:

1)

2)

3)

4)

What would I do differently from yesterday that my future self would thank me for?

Where did I win yesterday?

What are my three goals to accomplish today? If this is all I get accomplished today I will be happy and three steps closer towards my Primary Goal.

1)

2)

3)

"The best way to predict your future is to create it"

Daily Affirmations (as if you have already achieved it):

1)

2)

3)

WEEKLY REFLECTION

"We cannot become what we want by remaining what we are."

—Max Depree

Date: **Primary Goal:**

Weekly Goal Tracker

Week of: ....

Goal	Mon	Tue	Wed	Thu	Fri	Sat	Sun

Out of the goals you set last week, how many did you accomplish successfully?

.... / ....

Congratulations on the goals you accomplished successfully! You are that much closer to achieving your Primary Goal! Make sure you take the time to praise yourself for what you have accomplished and how far you have come.

Where did I win last week?

1) ....

2) ....

3) ....

4) ....

5) ....

How can I improve next week?

1) ....

2) ....

3) ....

4) ....

5) ....

"Never give up. You only get one life. Go for it!"

—RICHARD E. GRANT

WEEK THREE

Weekly Goals   **Primary Goal:**

Week:

Goals for this Week:

What goals do I want to accomplish this week to get me closer to my Primary Goal?

1. ....

2. ....

3. ....

4. ....

5. ....

6. ....

7. ....

You can document your weekly goals on your habit tracker pages at the end of every week to review your success.

Day 1/7

Date: **Primary Goal:**

> *"Focus on the journey, not the destination.*
> *Joy is found not in finishing an activity but in doing it."*

—GREG ANDERSON

Four things that I am grateful for:

1) ....

2) ....

3) ....

4) ....

What would I do differently from yesterday that my future self would thank me for?

....

Where did I win yesterday?

....

What are my three goals to accomplish today? If this is all I get accomplished today I will be happy and three steps closer towards my Primary Goal.

1) ....

2) ....

3) ....

> *"The best way to predict your future is to create it"*

Daily Affirmations (as if you have already achieved it):

1) ....

2) ....

3) ....

Day 2/7

Date: **Primary Goal:**

"Positivity, confidence, and persistence are key in life,
so never give up on yourself."

—KHALID

Four things that I am grateful for:

1) ....

2) ....

3) ....

4) ....

What would I do differently from yesterday that my future self would thank me for?

....

Where did I win yesterday?

....

What are my three goals to accomplish today? If this is all I get accomplished today I will be happy and three steps closer towards my Primary Goal.

1) ....

2) ....

3) ....

"The best way to predict your future is to create it"

Daily Affirmations (as if you have already achieved it):

1) ....

2) ....

3) ....

Day 3/7

Date: **Primary Goal:**

*"The greatest source of happiness is the ability
to be grateful at all times."*

—ZIG ZIGLAR

Four things that I am grateful for:

1)

2)

3)

4)

What would I do differently from yesterday that my future self would thank me for?

Where did I win yesterday?

What are my three goals to accomplish today? If this is all I get accomplished today I will be happy and three steps closer towards my Primary Goal.

1)

2)

3)

"The best way to predict your future is to create it"

Daily Affirmations (as if you have already achieved it):

1)

2)

3)

Day 4/7

Date: **Primary Goal:**

"The positive thinker sees the invisible,
feels the intangible, and achieves the impossible."

—WINSTON CHURCHILL

Four things that I am grateful for:

1) ....

2) ....

3) ....

4) ....

What would I do differently from yesterday that my future self would thank me for?

....

Where did I win yesterday?

....

What are my three goals to accomplish today? If this is all I get accomplished today I will be happy and three steps closer towards my Primary Goal.

1) ....

2) ....

3) ....

"The best way to predict your future is to create it"

Daily Affirmations (as if you have already achieved it):

1) ....

2) ....

3) ....

Day 5/7

Date: **Primary Goal:**

*"Enjoy the little things, for one day you may look back
and realize they were the big things."*

—ROBERT BRAULT

Four things that I am grateful for:

1) ....

2) ....

3) ....

4) ....

What would I do differently from yesterday that my future self would thank me for?

....

Where did I win yesterday?

....

What are my three goals to accomplish today? If this is all I get accomplished today I will be happy and three steps closer towards my Primary Goal.

1) ....

2) ....

3) ....

"The best way to predict your future is to create it"

Daily Affirmations (as if you have already achieved it):

1) ....

2) ....

3) ....

Day 6/7

> *"I don't focus on what I'm up against.*
> *I focus on my goals and I try to ignore the rest."*
>
> —VENUS WILLIAMS

Four things that I am grateful for:

1) ....

2) ....

3) ....

4) ....

What would I do differently from yesterday that my future self would thank me for?

....

Where did I win yesterday?

....

What are my three goals to accomplish today? If this is all I get accomplished today I will be happy and three steps closer towards my Primary Goal.

1) ....

2) ....

3) ....

> *"The best way to predict your future is to create it"*

Daily Affirmations (as if you have already achieved it):

1) ....

2) ....

3) ....

Day 7/7

Date: **Primary Goal:**

"I think goals should never be easy, they should force you to work,
even if they are uncomfortable at the time."

—MICHAEL PHELPS

Four things that I am grateful for:

1) ....

2) ....

3) ....

4) ....

What would I do differently from yesterday that my future self would thank me for?

....

Where did I win yesterday?

....

What are my three goals to accomplish today? If this is all I get accomplished today I will be happy and three steps closer towards my Primary Goal.

1) ....

2) ....

3) ....

"The best way to predict your future is to create it"

Daily Affirmations (as if you have already achieved it):

1) ....

2) ....

3) ....

WEEKLY REFLECTION

"We cannot become what we want by remaining what we are."

—MAX DEPREE

Date: **Primary Goal:**

WEEKLY GOAL TRACKER

Week of: ....

Goal	Mon	Tue	Wed	Thu	Fri	Sat	Sun

Out of the goals you set last week, how many did you accomplish successfully?

.... / ....

Congratulations on the goals you accomplished successfully! You are that much closer to achieving your Primary Goal! Make sure you take the time to praise yourself for what you have accomplished and how far you have come.

Where did I win last week?

1) ....

2) ....

3) ....

4) ....

5) ....

How can I improve next week?

1) ....

2) ....

3) ....

4) ....

5) ....

"Success is steady progress toward one's personal goals."

—Jim Rohn

WEEK FOUR

Weekly Goals   **Primary Goal:**

Week:

Goals for this Week:

What goals do I want to accomplish this week to get me closer to my Primary Goal?

1. ....

2. ....

3. ....

4. ....

5. ....

6. ....

7. ....

You can document your weekly goals on your habit tracker pages at the end of every week to review your success.

Day 1/7

Date: **Primary Goal:**

> *"Setting goals is the first step in turning the invisible into the visible."*
>
> —TONY ROBBINS

Four things that I am grateful for:

1) ....

2) ....

3) ....

4) ....

What would I do differently from yesterday that my future self would thank me for?

....

Where did I win yesterday?

....

What are my three goals to accomplish today? If this is all I get accomplished today I will be happy and three steps closer towards my Primary Goal.

1) ....

2) ....

3) ....

> *"The best way to predict your future is to create it"*

Daily Affirmations (as if you have already achieved it):

1) ....

2) ....

3) ....

Day 2/7

Date: **Primary Goal:**

*"Wear gratitude like a cloak, and it will feed
every corner of your life."*

—RUMI

Four things that I am grateful for:

1) ....

2) ....

3)...

4)...

What would I do differently from yesterday that my future self would
thank me for?

....

Where did I win yesterday?

....

What are my three goals to accomplish today? If this is all I get accomplished
today I will be happy and three steps closer towards my Primary Goal.

1) ....

2) ....

3) ....

"The best way to predict your future is to create it"

Daily Affirmations (as if you have already achieved it):

1) ....

2) ....

3) ....

Day 3/7

Date: **Primary Goal:**

"One of the lessons that I grew up with was to always stay true to yourself and never let what somebody else says distract you from your goals. And so when I hear about negative and false attacks, I really don't invest any energy in them, because I know who I am."

—MICHELLE OBAMA

Four things that I am grateful for:

1) ....

2) ....

3) ....

4) ....

What would I do differently from yesterday that my future self would thank me for?

....

Where did I win yesterday?

....

What are my three goals to accomplish today? If this is all I get accomplished today I will be happy and three steps closer towards my Primary Goal.

1) ....

2) ....

3) ....

"The best way to predict your future is to create it"

Daily Affirmations (as if you have already achieved it):

1) ....

2) ....

3) ....

Day 4/7

Date: **Primary Goal:**

"Success is the sum of small efforts—
repeated day in and day out."

—ROBERT COLLIER

Four things that I am grateful for:

1) ....

2) ....

3) ....

4) ....

What would I do differently from yesterday that my future self would thank me for?

....

Where did I win yesterday?

....

What are my three goals to accomplish today? If this is all I get accomplished today I will be happy and three steps closer towards my Primary Goal.

1) ....

2) ....

3) ....

"The best way to predict your future is to create it"

Daily Affirmations (as if you have already achieved it):

1) ....

2) ....

3) ....

Day 5/7

Date: **Primary Goal:**

"No one has the power to shatter your dreams
unless you give it to them."

—MAEVE GREYSON

Four things that I am grateful for:

1) ....

2) ....

3) ....

4) ....

What would I do differently from yesterday that my future self would thank me for?

....

Where did I win yesterday?

....

What are my three goals to accomplish today? If this is all I get accomplished today I will be happy and three steps closer towards my Primary Goal.

1) ....

2) ....

3) ....

"The best way to predict your future is to create it"

Daily Affirmations (as if you have already achieved it):

1) ....

2) ....

3) ....

Day 6/7

Date: **Primary Goal:**

"Change your thoughts and you change your world."

—NORMAN VINCENT PEALE

Four things that I am grateful for:

1) ....

2) ....

3) ....

4) ....

What would I do differently from yesterday that my future self would thank me for?

....

Where did I win yesterday?

....

What are my three goals to accomplish today? If this is all I get accomplished today I will be happy and three steps closer towards my Primary Goal.

1) ....

2) ....

3) ....

"The best way to predict your future is to create it"

Daily Affirmations (as if you have already achieved it):

1) ....

2) ....

3) ....

Day 7/7

Date: **Primary Goal:**

"When I was 5 years old, my mother always told me that happiness was the key to life. When I went to school, they asked me what I wanted to be when I grew up. I wrote down 'happy'. They told me I didn't understand the assignment, and I told them they didn't understand life."

—JOHN LENNON

Four things that I am grateful for:

1)
2)
3)
4)

What would I do differently from yesterday that my future self would thank me for?

Where did I win yesterday?

What are my three goals to accomplish today? If this is all I get accomplished today I will be happy and three steps closer towards my Primary Goal.

1)
2)
3)

"The best way to predict your future is to create it"

Daily Affirmations (as if you have already achieved it):

1)
2)
3)

WEEKLY REFLECTION

"We cannot become what we want by remaining what we are."

—MAX DEPREE

Date: **Primary Goal:**

WEEKLY GOAL TRACKER

Week of: ....

Goal	Mon	Tue	Wed	Thu	Fri	Sat	Sun

Out of the goals you set last week, how many did you accomplish successfully?

.... / ....

Congratulations on the goals you accomplished successfully! You are that much closer to achieving your Primary Goal! Make sure you take the time to praise yourself for what you have accomplished and how far you have come.

Where did I win last week?

1) ....

2) ....

3) ....

4) ....

5) ....

How can I improve next week?

1) ....

2) ....

3) ....

4) ....

5) ....

"Permanence, perseverance and persistence in spite of all obstacles, discouragements, and impossibilities: It is this, that in all things distinguishes the strong soul from the weak."

—THOMAS CARLYLE

MONTH:

Date   **Primary Goal:**

Month:

Goals for this Month:

HEALTH & FITNESS

1.
2.
3.
4.
5.

FINANCE

1.
2.
3.
4.
5.

RELATIONSHIPS

1.
2.
3.
4.
5.

CAREER

1.
2.
3.
4.
5.

OTHER

1.
2.
3.
4.
5.

WEEK ONE

Weekly Goals   **Primary Goal:**

Week:
Goals for this Week:

What goals do I want to accomplish this week to get me closer to my Primary Goal?

1. ....

2. ....

3. ....

4. ....

5. ....

6. ....

7. ....

You can document your weekly goals on your habit tracker pages at the end of every week to review your success.

Day 1/7

Date: **Primary Goal:**

*"People with goals succeed because
they know where they're going."*

—EARL NIGHTINGALE

Four things that I am grateful for:

1) ....

2) ....

3) ....

4) ....

What would I do differently from yesterday that my future self would thank me for?

....

Where did I win yesterday?

....

What are my three goals to accomplish today? If this is all I get accomplished today I will be happy and three steps closer towards my Primary Goal.

1) ....

2) ....

3) ....

"The best way to predict your future is to create it"

Daily Affirmations (as if you have already achieved it):

1) ....

2) ....

3) ....

Day 2/7

Date: **Primary Goal:**

*"When I started counting my blessings,
my whole life turned around."*

—WILLIE NELSON

Four things that I am grateful for:

1) ....

2) ....

3) ....

4) ....

What would I do differently from yesterday that my future self would
thank me for?

....

Where did I win yesterday?

....

What are my three goals to accomplish today? If this is all I get accomplished
today I will be happy and three steps closer towards my Primary Goal.

1) ....

2) ....

3) ....

"The best way to predict your future is to create it"

Daily Affirmations (as if you have already achieved it):

1) ....

2) ....

3) ....

Day 3/7

Date: **Primary Goal:**

*"Discipline is the bridge between goals
and accomplishment."*

—JIM ROHN

Four things that I am grateful for:

1) ....

2) ....

3) ....

4) ....

What would I do differently from yesterday that my future self would thank me for?

....

Where did I win yesterday?

....

What are my three goals to accomplish today? If this is all I get accomplished today I will be happy and three steps closer towards my Primary Goal.

1) ....

2) ....

3) ....

"The best way to predict your future is to create it"

Daily Affirmations (as if you have already achieved it):

1) ....

2) ....

3) ....

Day 4/7

Date: **Primary Goal:**

> *"Whether you think you can or you think you can't,*
> *you're right."*
>
> —HENRY FORD

Four things that I am grateful for:

1) ....

2) ....

3) ....

4) ....

What would I do differently from yesterday that my future self would thank me for?

....

Where did I win yesterday?

....

What are my three goals to accomplish today? If this is all I get accomplished today I will be happy and three steps closer towards my Primary Goal.

1) ....

2) ....

3) ....

> *"The best way to predict your future is to create it"*

Daily Affirmations (as if you have already achieved it):

1) ....

2) ....

3) ....

Day 5/7

Date: **Primary Goal:**

"Eighty percent of success is showing up."

—WOODY ALLEN

Four things that I am grateful for:

1) ....

2) ....

3) ....

4) ....

What would I do differently from yesterday that my future self would thank me for?

....

Where did I win yesterday?

....

What are my three goals to accomplish today? If this is all I get accomplished today I will be happy and three steps closer towards my Primary Goal.

1) ....

2) ....

3) ....

"The best way to predict your future is to create it"

Daily Affirmations (as if you have already achieved it):

1) ....

2) ....

3) ....

Date: **Primary Goal:**

"Much of the stress that people feel doesn't come from having too much to do. It comes from not finishing what they've started."

—DAVID ALLEN

Four things that I am grateful for:

1) ....

2) ....

3) ....

4) ....

What would I do differently from yesterday that my future self would thank me for?

....

Where did I win yesterday?

....

What are my three goals to accomplish today? If this is all I get accomplished today I will be happy and three steps closer towards my Primary Goal.

1) ....

2) ....

3) ....

"The best way to predict your future is to create it"

Daily Affirmations (as if you have already achieved it):

1) ....

2) ....

3) ....

Day 7/7

Date: **Primary Goal:**

"The one thing you've gotta do is that you need to always do the best you can do, no matter what the given situation, no matter what comes up against you. You do the best you can do, and you never give up. Never quit."

—JAMES CORDEN

Four things that I am grateful for:

1) ....

2) ....

3) ....

4) ....

What would I do differently from yesterday that my future self would thank me for?

....

Where did I win yesterday?

....

What are my three goals to accomplish today? If this is all I get accomplished today I will be happy and three steps closer towards my Primary Goal.

1) ....

2) ....

3) ....

"The best way to predict your future is to create it"

Daily Affirmations (as if you have already achieved it):

1) ....

2) ....

3) ....

WEEKLY REFLECTION

"We cannot become what we want by remaining what we are."

—Max Depree

Date: **Primary Goal:**

WEEKLY GOAL TRACKER

Week of: ....

Goal	Mon	Tue	Wed	Thu	Fri	Sat	Sun

Out of the goals you set last week, how many did you accomplish successfully?

.... / ....

Congratulations on the goals you accomplished successfully! You are that much closer to achieving your Primary Goal! Make sure you take the time to praise yourself for what you have accomplished and how far you have come.

Where did I win last week?

1) ....

2) ....

3) ....

4) ....

5) ....

How can I improve next week?

1) ....

2) ....

3) ....

4) ....

5) ....

"Your goals are the road maps that guide you and show you what is possible for your life."

—LES BROWN

WEEK TWO

Weekly Goals   **Primary Goal:**

Week:
Goals for this Week:

What goals do I want to accomplish this week to get me closer to my Primary Goal?

1. ....

2. ....

3. ....

4. ....

5. ....

6. ....

7. ....

You can document your weekly goals on your habit tracker pages at the end of every week to review your success.

Day 1/7

Date: **Primary Goal:**

"Success is not final, failure is not fatal:
it is the courage to continue that counts."

—WINSTON CHURCHILL

Four things that I am grateful for:

1) ....

2) ....

3) ....

4) ....

What would I do differently from yesterday that my future self would thank me for?

....

Where did I win yesterday?

....

What are my three goals to accomplish today? If this is all I get accomplished today I will be happy and three steps closer towards my Primary Goal.

1) ....

2) ....

3) ....

"The best way to predict your future is to create it"

Daily Affirmations (as if you have already achieved it):

1) ....

2) ....

3) ....

Day 2/7

Date: **Primary Goal:**

"Action is the foundational key to all success."

—PABLO PICASSO

Four things that I am grateful for:

1) ....

2) ....

3) ....

4) ....

What would I do differently from yesterday that my future self would thank me for?

....

Where did I win yesterday?

....

What are my three goals to accomplish today? If this is all I get accomplished today I will be happy and three steps closer towards my Primary Goal.

1) ....

2) ....

3) ....

"The best way to predict your future is to create it"

Daily Affirmations (as if you have already achieved it):

1) ....

2) ....

3) ....

Day 3/7

Date: **Primary Goal:**

> *"Gratitude is a powerful catalyst for happiness.
> It's the spark that lights a fire of joy in your soul."*
>
> —AMY COLLETTE

Four things that I am grateful for:

1) ....

2) ....

3) ....

4) ....

What would I do differently from yesterday that my future self would thank me for?

....

Where did I win yesterday?

....

What are my three goals to accomplish today? If this is all I get accomplished today I will be happy and three steps closer towards my Primary Goal.

1) ....

2) ....

3) ....

> *"The best way to predict your future is to create it"*

Daily Affirmations (as if you have already achieved it):

1) ....

2) ....

3) ....

Day 4/7

Date: **Primary Goal:**

"Gratitude for the present moment and the fullness of life now is the true prosperity."

—ECKHART TOLLE

Four things that I am grateful for:

1) ....

2) ....

3) ....

4) ....

What would I do differently from yesterday that my future self would thank me for?

....

Where did I win yesterday?

....

What are my three goals to accomplish today? If this is all I get accomplished today I will be happy and three steps closer towards my Primary Goal.

1) ....

2) ....

3) ....

"The best way to predict your future is to create it"

Daily Affirmations (as if you have already achieved it):

1) ....

2) ....

3) ....

Day 5/7

Date: **Primary Goal:**

"We love to commiserate and troubleshoot and prepare for the worst, and gratitude yanks us out of that and reminds us of the ridiculous amount of infinite blessings that are around us at all times."

—JEN SINCERO

Four things that I am grateful for:

1) ....

2) ....

3) ....

4) ....

What would I do differently from yesterday that my future self would thank me for?

....

Where did I win yesterday?

....

What are my three goals to accomplish today? If this is all I get accomplished today I will be happy and three steps closer towards my Primary Goal.

1) ....

2) ....

3) ....

"The best way to predict your future is to create it"

Daily Affirmations (as if you have already achieved it):

1) ....

2) ....

3) ....

Day 6/7

Date: **Primary Goal:**

It is never too late to be what you might have been.

—GEORGE ELIOT

Four things that I am grateful for:

1) ....

2) ....

3) ....

4) ....

What would I do differently from yesterday that my future self would thank me for?

....

Where did I win yesterday?

....

What are my three goals to accomplish today? If this is all I get accomplished today I will be happy and three steps closer towards my Primary Goal.

1) ....

2) ....

3) ....

"The best way to predict your future is to create it"

Daily Affirmations (as if you have already achieved it):

1) ....

2) ....

3) ....

Day 7/7

Date: **Primary Goal:**

> *"I hated every minute of training, but I said, 'Don't quit.*
> *Suffer now and live the rest of your life as a champion.'"*
>
> —MUHAMMAD ALI

Four things that I am grateful for:

1) ....

2) ....

3) ....

4) ....

What would I do differently from yesterday that my future self would thank me for?

....

Where did I win yesterday?

....

What are my three goals to accomplish today? If this is all I get accomplished today I will be happy and three steps closer towards my Primary Goal.

1) ....

2) ....

3) ....

> *"The best way to predict your future is to create it"*

Daily Affirmations (as if you have already achieved it):

1) ....

2) ....

3) ....

WEEKLY REFLECTION

"We cannot become what we want by remaining what we are."

—Max Depree

Date: **Primary Goal:**

Weekly Goal Tracker

Week of: ....

Goal	Mon	Tue	Wed	Thu	Fri	Sat	Sun

Out of the goals you set last week, how many did you accomplish successfully?

.... / ....

Congratulations on the goals you accomplished successfully! You are that much closer to achieving your Primary Goal! Make sure you take the time to praise yourself for what you have accomplished and how far you have come.

Where did I win last week?

1)

2)

3)

4)

5)

How can I improve next week?

1)

2)

3)

4)

5)

"Light tomorrow with today!"
—Elizabeth Barrett Browning

Reminder:

You have two weeks left of this Gratitude Journal and we recommend you order your next Gratitude Journal.

For more information or to place an order, please email winthedayjournal@gmail.com

or follow me on Instagram at @winthedayjournal

WEEK THREE

Weekly Goals   **Primary Goal:**

Week:

Goals for this Week:

What goals do I want to accomplish this week to get me closer to my Primary Goal?

1. ....

2. ....

3. ....

4. ....

5. ....

6. ....

7. ....

You can document your weekly goals on your habit tracker pages at the end of every week to review your success.

Day 1/7

Date: **Primary Goal:**

"Whatever we are waiting for —peace of mind, contentment, grace, the inner awareness of simple abundance —it will surely come to us, but only when we are ready to receive it with an open and grateful heart."

—SARAH BAN BREATHNACH

Four things that I am grateful for:

1) ....
2) ....
3) ....
4) ....

What would I do differently from yesterday that my future self would thank me for?

....

Where did I win yesterday?

....

What are my three goals to accomplish today? If this is all I get accomplished today I will be happy and three steps closer towards my Primary Goal.

1) ....
2) ....
3) ....

"The best way to predict your future is to create it"

Daily Affirmations (as if you have already achieved it):

1) ....
2) ....
3) ....

Day 2/7

"I am not the richest, smartest or most talented person in the world, but I succeed because I keep going and going and going."

—SYLVESTER STALLONE

Four things that I am grateful for:

1) ....

2) ....

3) ....

4) ....

What would I do differently from yesterday that my future self would thank me for?

....

Where did I win yesterday?

....

What are my three goals to accomplish today? If this is all I get accomplished today I will be happy and three steps closer towards my Primary Goal.

1) ....

2) ....

3) ....

"The best way to predict your future is to create it"

Daily Affirmations (as if you have already achieved it):

1) ....

2) ....

3) ....

Day 3/7

Date: **Primary Goal:**

*"Motivation is what gets you started.
Habit is what keeps you going."*

—JIM ROHN

Four things that I am grateful for:

1) ....

2) ....

3) ....

4) ....

What would I do differently from yesterday that my future self would thank me for?

....

Where did I win yesterday?

....

What are my three goals to accomplish today? If this is all I get accomplished today I will be happy and three steps closer towards my Primary Goal.

1) ....

2) ....

3) ....

"The best way to predict your future is to create it"

Daily Affirmations (as if you have already achieved it):

1) ....

2) ....

3) ....

Day 4/7

Date: **Primary Goal:**

*"The best preparation for tomorrow
is doing your best today."*

—H. JACKSON BROWN, JR.

Four things that I am grateful for:

1)

2)

3)

4)

What would I do differently from yesterday that my future self would thank me for?

Where did I win yesterday?

What are my three goals to accomplish today? If this is all I get accomplished today I will be happy and three steps closer towards my Primary Goal.

1)

2)

3)

"The best way to predict your future is to create it"

Daily Affirmations (as if you have already achieved it):

1)

2)

3)

Day 5/7

Date: **Primary Goal:**

*"Don't judge each day by the harvest you reap
but by the seeds that you plant."*

—ROBERT LOUIS STEVENSON

Four things that I am grateful for:

1) ....

2) ....

3) ....

4) ....

What would I do differently from yesterday that my future self would thank me for?

....

Where did I win yesterday?

....

What are my three goals to accomplish today? If this is all I get accomplished today I will be happy and three steps closer towards my Primary Goal.

1) ....

2) ....

3) ....

"The best way to predict your future is to create it"

Daily Affirmations (as if you have already achieved it):

1) ....

2) ....

3) ....

Day 6/7

Date: **Primary Goal:**

*"Choosing to be positive and having a grateful attitude
is going to determine how you're going to live your life."*

—JOEL OSTEEN

Four things that I am grateful for:

1) ....

2) ....

3) ....

4) ....

What would I do differently from yesterday that my future self would thank me for?

....

Where did I win yesterday?

....

What are my three goals to accomplish today? If this is all I get accomplished today I will be happy and three steps closer towards my Primary Goal.

1) ....

2) ....

3) ....

"The best way to predict your future is to create it"

Daily Affirmations (as if you have already achieved it):

1) ....

2) ....

3) ....

Day 7/7

Date: **Primary Goal:**

"You just do it. You force yourself to get up. You force yourself to put one foot before the other, and God damn it, you refuse to let it get to you. You fight. You cry. You curse. Then you go about the business of living. That's how I've done it. There's no other way."

—ELIZABETH TAYLOR

Four things that I am grateful for:

1) ....

2) ....

3) ....

4) ....

What would I do differently from yesterday that my future self would thank me for?

....

Where did I win yesterday?

....

What are my three goals to accomplish today? If this is all I get accomplished today I will be happy and three steps closer towards my Primary Goal.

1) ....

2) ....

3) ....

"The best way to predict your future is to create it"

Daily Affirmations (as if you have already achieved it):

1) ....

2) ....

3) ....

WEEKLY REFLECTION

"We cannot become what we want by remaining what we are."

—Max Depree

Date: **Primary Goal:**

WEEKLY GOAL TRACKER

Week of: ....

Goal	Mon	Tue	Wed	Thu	Fri	Sat	Sun

Out of the goals you set last week, how many did you accomplish successfully?

.... / ....

Congratulations on the goals you accomplished successfully! You are that much closer to achieving your Primary Goal! Make sure you take the time to praise yourself for what you have accomplished and how far you have come.

Where did I win last week?

1)

2)

3)

4)

5)

How can I improve next week?

1)

2)

3)

4)

5)

*"Do today what others won't
so tomorrow you can do what others can't."*

—JERRY RICE

WEEK FOUR

Weekly Goals   **Primary Goal:**

Week:
Goals for this Week:

What goals do I want to accomplish this week to get me closer to my Primary Goal?

1. ....

2. ....

3. ....

4. ....

5. ....

6. ....

7. ....

You can document your weekly goals on your habit tracker pages at the end of every week to review your success.

Day 1/7

Date: **Primary Goal:**

*"Start by doing what's necessary; then do what's possible;
and suddenly you are doing the impossible."*

—FRANCIS OF ASSISI

Four things that I am grateful for:

1) ....

2) ....

3) ....

4) ....

What would I do differently from yesterday that my future self would thank me for?

....

Where did I win yesterday?

....

What are my three goals to accomplish today? If this is all I get accomplished today I will be happy and three steps closer towards my Primary Goal.

1) ....

2) ....

3) ....

"The best way to predict your future is to create it"

Daily Affirmations (as if you have already achieved it):

1) ....

2) ....

3) ....

Day 2/7

Date: **Primary Goal:**

"What lies behind you and what lies in front of you,
pales in comparison to what lies inside of you."

—Ralph Waldo Emerson

Four things that I am grateful for:

1)

2)

3)

4)

What would I do differently from yesterday that my future self would thank me for?

Where did I win yesterday?

What are my three goals to accomplish today? If this is all I get accomplished today I will be happy and three steps closer towards my Primary Goal.

1)

2)

3)

"The best way to predict your future is to create it"

Daily Affirmations (as if you have already achieved it):

1)

2)

3)

Day 3/7

Date: **Primary Goal:**

"It is always the simple that produces the marvelous."

—AMELIA BARR

Four things that I am grateful for:

1) ....

2) ....

3) ....

4) ....

What would I do differently from yesterday that my future self would thank me for?

....

Where did I win yesterday?

....

What are my three goals to accomplish today? If this is all I get accomplished today I will be happy and three steps closer towards my Primary Goal.

1) ....

2) ....

3) ....

"The best way to predict your future is to create it"

Daily Affirmations (as if you have already achieved it):

1) ....

2) ....

3) ....

Day 4/7

Date: **Primary Goal:**

"When you are grateful —when you can see what you have —
you unlock blessings to flow in your life."

—SUZE ORMAN

Four things that I am grateful for:

1) ....

2) ....

3) ....

4) ....

What would I do differently from yesterday that my future self would thank me for?

....

Where did I win yesterday?

....

What are my three goals to accomplish today? If this is all I get accomplished today I will be happy and three steps closer towards my Primary Goal.

1) ....

2) ....

3) ....

"The best way to predict your future is to create it"

Daily Affirmations (as if you have already achieved it):

1) ....

2) ....

3) ....

Day 5/7

Date: **Primary Goal:**

"It's not possible to experience constant euphoria,
but if you're grateful, you can find happiness in everything."

—PHARRELL WILLIAMS

Four things that I am grateful for:

1) ....

2) ....

3) ....

4) ....

What would I do differently from yesterday that my future self would thank me for?

....

Where did I win yesterday?

....

What are my three goals to accomplish today? If this is all I get accomplished today I will be happy and three steps closer towards my Primary Goal.

1) ....

2) ....

3) ....

"The best way to predict your future is to create it"

Daily Affirmations (as if you have already achieved it):

1) ....

2) ....

3) ....

Date: **Primary Goal:**

> *"When you are grateful, fear disappears and abundance appears."*
> —ANTHONY ROBBINS

Four things that I am grateful for:

1) ....

2) ....

3) ....

4) ....

What would I do differently from yesterday that my future self would thank me for?

....

Where did I win yesterday?

....

What are my three goals to accomplish today? If this is all I get accomplished today I will be happy and three steps closer towards my Primary Goal.

1) ....

2) ....

3) ....

> *"The best way to predict your future is to create it"*

Daily Affirmations (as if you have already achieved it):

1) ....

2) ....

3) ....

Day 7/7

Date: **Primary Goal:**

> *"Believe in yourself and all that you are, know that there is something inside you that is greater than any obstacle."*
>
> —CHRISTIAN D. LARSON

Four things that I am grateful for:

1) ....

2) ....

3) ....

4) ....

What would I do differently from yesterday that my future self would thank me for?

....

Where did I win yesterday?

....

What are my three goals to accomplish today? If this is all I get accomplished today I will be happy and three steps closer towards my Primary Goal.

1) ....

2) ....

3) ....

> *"The best way to predict your future is to create it"*

Daily Affirmations (as if you have already achieved it):

1) ....

2) ....

3) ....

WEEKLY REFLECTION

"We cannot become what we want by remaining what we are."

—Max Depree

Date: **Primary Goal:**

Weekly Goal Tracker

Week of: ....

Goal	Mon	Tue	Wed	Thu	Fri	Sat	Sun

Out of the goals you set last week, how many did you accomplish successfully?

.... / ....

Congratulations on the goals you accomplished successfully! You are that much closer to achieving your Primary Goal! Make sure you take the time to praise yourself for what you have accomplished and how far you have come.

Where did I win last week?

1) ....

2) ....

3) ....

4) ....

5) ....

How can I improve next week?

1) ....

2) ....

3) ....

4) ....

5) ....

"Your victory is right around the corner. Never give up."

—Nicki Minaj

Congratulations on the completion of your Win the Morning, Win the Day Gratitude Journal! I hope you enjoyed the journey and found success in the process. Take this opportunity to reflect on your progress and celebrate your accomplishments.

Goals Achieved During the last 4 Months:

1) ....

2) ....

3) ....

4) ....

5) ....

For more information or to place an order,
please email
winthedayjournal@gmail.com

or follow me on Instagram at
@winthedayjournal

ACKNOWLEDGMENTS

This journal is a reflection of my supportive family and friends, who inspire me to pursue my dreams to the fullest while also enjoying the process along the way.

To my partner Taylor, thank you for your endless encouragement, motivation to never give up and for being the person I look up to everyday.

To the strong women who helped me create this successful strategy by putting it to work and seeing the results first hand, thank you. Chelsie, Jenna and Sylvia your motivation and outlook on life is contagious and without it this journal would not be a reality.